The Essence of Julian

A Paraphrase of Julian of Norwich's
Revelations of Divine Love

Other books by Ralph Milton

Radio Broadcasting for Developing Nations
The Gift of Story
Through Rose-colored Bifocals
This United Church of Ours
Commonsense Christianity
Is This Your Idea of a Good Time, God?
God for Beginners
Living God's Way
The Family Story Bible
Man to Man
How to Write and Publish Your Church History
Sermon Seasonings
Angels in Red Suspenders

and most recently the historical novel

Julian's Cell: An Earthy Story of Julian of Norwich

RALPH MILTON

E THE ssence OF Julian

A Paraphrase of Julian of Norwich's
Revelations of Divine Love

Northstone

Editor: Michael Schwartzentruber
Cover and interior design: Margaret Kyle
Cover artwork: Hillarie Cornwell, copyright 2002 © Cornwell ScribeWorks, Chico, CA,
scribewrks@aol.com. Used by permission.
Author photo: Wayne E. Duchart, Photography West, Kelowna, B.C.
Proofreading: Dianne Greenslade

Northstone Publishing acknowledges the financial support of the Government of Canada
through the Book Publishing Industry Development Program for its publishing activities.

Northstone Publishing is an imprint of Wood Lake Books Inc., an employee-owned company,
and is committed to caring for the environment and all creation. Northstone recycles and reuses
and encourages readers to do the same. Resources are printed on recycled paper and more
environmentally friendly groundwood papers (newsprint), whenever possible. The trees used are
replaced through donations to the Scoutrees For Canada Program. A portion of all profit is donated
to charitable organizations.

National Library of Canada Cataloguing in Publication Data
Julian of Norwich, b. 1343
[Revelations of divine love. English]
The essence of Julian
ISBN 1-896836-52-6
1. Julian, of Norwich, b. 1343. 2. Devotional literature, English
(Middle) I. Title. II. Title: Essence of Julian.
BV4831.J813 2002   248.2'2   C2002-910652-4

Published by Northstone Publishing,
an imprint of Wood Lake Books Inc.
Kelowna, British Columbia, Canada
www.joinhands.com

Printing 10 9 8 7 6 5 4 3 2 1
Printed in Canada at Transcontinental Printing

To
The Friends of Julian,
an international organization
that has helped so many of us
know and love
the holy woman we call
Julian of Norwich

You have made us for Yourself, O God,
and our hearts are restless till they rest in You.

St. Augustine of Hippo

Dare I add, O my God,
that Your Heart is restless until it rests in me?

Gerald Serafin

Preface

When I fell in love with Julian of Norwich a number of years ago, I had no idea where it would lead. In the first flush of my fascination with this woman who lived 600 years ago, it didn't occur to me that her book, which was praised by so many people, would be a tough read. *Revelations of Divine Love* is deceptively simple. I would read a chapter or two, which seemed clear enough, then suddenly find myself completely baffled.

Trying to read her own medieval English words, I often had no idea what she was saying. Even in translation into modern English, she was difficult. So I was heartened to read in the foreword to *Julian of Norwich – Showings* by Edmund Colledge and James Walsh that even these two eminent Julian scholars found that "Julian is tough going!"

Preparing to write my historical novel *Julian's Cell*, I read Julian's book probably a dozen times in several modern translations. I even undertook my own, very rough, translation. All of this was more difficult than I expected.

In my enthusiasm about Julian, I convinced a number of friends and family to read her book. Several of them gave up after a few chapters, even though they had degrees in theology. That is when I decided that many of us need a "leg up" to read and understand this remarkable woman.

The book you are holding in your hands is both a paraphrase and a condensation. By paraphrasing Julian's words into modern

colloquial English, I've tried to translate not just her words but her ideas into contemporary, casual language. And I have condensed Julian's book to less than half its original length.

Julian writes out of her medieval world, and some of her ideas are very difficult, perhaps impossible, for most moderns to understand. She also gets a bit wordy and occasionally repeats herself. I felt a shorter book would be more useful to busy people who simply want an introduction to her thinking.

Not everyone will be happy with what I have done. Some Julian scholars will tell you that I have left out some important parts. They will be right.

Others will disagree with my interpretation of what she wrote. That is as it should be. We read the works of a spiritual giant such as Julian out of our own need. In Julian's book, as in other great books, there is such an abundance of riches that we can each find what we hunger for.

You will notice that I have centered some of the passages to highlight the poetry that runs through Julian's prose. This is my doing, not Julian's; 14th-century writers didn't even use paragraph indentations.

I sincerely hope that this paraphrased, condensed version of Julian's book will make you hunger for more. If you've not read it already, a next step might be my historical novel about her life – *Julian's Cell: An Earthy Story of Julian of Norwich*. At the back of that book you will find a list of other translations and other resources you can use to grow in your understanding.

This book, *The Essence of Julian*, begins with a short introduction to some of the circumstances of Julian's life, which I hope will help you understand her work. If you already know a fair bit about Julian, you could skip that and go directly to the paraphrase.

I hope you will be inspired by her as much as I have been.

Introduction

Who was Julian of Norwich?

First of all, her name wasn't Julian. We don't know what her name was. In fact, the things we know for sure about the woman who wrote this fine book can be told in a few short paragraphs.

The person we call Julian of Norwich was born in 1342, the same year as Geoffrey Chaucer. When she was 30 years old, she had a very serious illness during which she experienced a series of visions. Her mother and some other people were there during her illness. She wrote two accounts of that experience. The first one, known as the *Short Text*, was probably written soon after her visions, and the second one, which we call the *Long Text*, was written some 20 years later. It was the first book written by a woman in the English language. It is this *Long Text* that you find paraphrased and abridged in this book.

At some point Julian became an anchorite attached to the church of Saint Julian in Norwich, from which she took her name. We think she was still alive in 1414 because her name is mentioned in a will. She would have been in her early 70s, very old for the 14th century.

Julian doesn't say much about herself because she wants us to pay attention to what she wrote. Even so, it has been my experience, and the experience of many others, that her writings take on depth and significance if we know a bit about her time and circumstances.

Over a period of four years, as I worked on the historical novel

Julian's Cell, I became more and more astonished at her writing. How could she write about such a gentle, loving God, when her church preached such a terrifying, angry God? Gradually, I discovered what an exceptional person she was. More than that, she ministered to my soul in a powerful and tender way, for which I am profoundly grateful.

Julian was an anchorite. That is *not* what makes her exceptional. There were many anchorites in England during her time. But it seems a strange vocation from our modern perspective.

An anchorite was permanently enclosed in a room, usually attached to a church. She (or he) took a vow to remain in that anchorhold until death. The ceremony which the bishop used to enclose an anchorite was the liturgy used to bury the dead. There were absolutely no circumstances under which she could leave that cell.

The anchorite would be committed to a life of prayer and counsel. The prayer life was usually patterned around the Benedictine Rule, which called for seven periods of prayer during the course of the day and night. That worked out to about four hours a day on her knees. Prayer was at the center of her vocation as an anchorite.

In addition, the anchorite had a window to the street, through which she would offer counseling to whoever approached her. Julian and the other anchorites were the forerunners of today's psychiatrists, social workers, and pastoral counselors.

We have only one report from a visitor to Julian's cell. Marjorie Kempe, of King's Lynne, writes of her visit to Julian in 1413. We know that anchorites were highly regarded as counselors because we have accounts of other visits to anchorites. For instance, the boy king, Richard II, visited an anchorite in London on his way to quell the Peasants' Revolt of 1381. We think Julian was held in high regard by the people of Norwich because she is mentioned in several wills.

There was no "order" of anchorites, as there were orders for priests, monks, and nuns. Anchorites could be male or female. They could be lay, clergy, or monk if they were male. They could be nun or laywoman if they were female. We don't know if Julian was a nun or perhaps a Beguine.* The question is passionately argued by many. We *do* know that she would have had some connection with Carrow Abbey, a convent just a few minutes walk from her anchorhold, because that abbey owned St. Julian's Church.

Personally, I think she was a laywoman and had been a mother, but that is simply an impression I have from reading her book. That is how she lives in my imagination and so that is how I presented her in my book *Julian's Cell.* There is no hard evidence, one way or the other. Nor do we know at what point in her life she became an anchorite.

Julian's book is an astonishing document considering the times in which she lived and the way it speaks so clearly to our own time. Historian Barbara Tushman called this era "the calamitous 14th century."

When Julian was six years old, the plague that we now call the "Black Death" swept through Europe. It killed a third to half of the people. Julian would almost certainly have lost family and friends in that plague. It came back twice more during her lifetime – the second onslaught killing mostly children who had not developed immunity during the previous wave. It is quite possible that Julian would have lost infants of her own in this "children's pestilence." There were also crop failures and cattle diseases, all of which added to the general misery of the people of England, especially the serfs at the bottom of the social ladder.

*BEGUINES WERE AN INFORMAL GATHERING OF WOMEN WHO DEVOTED THEMSELVES TO PRAYER AND GOOD WORKS. THEY WERE NOT MEMBERS OF A RELIGIOUS ORDER AND COULD LEAVE THEIR COMMUNITY OF WOMEN AND GO BACK TO SECULAR LIVES WHENEVER THEY CHOSE, AND WITHOUT BLAME. THE BEGUINES, VERY STRONG ACROSS THE ENGLISH CHANNEL, ONLY HAD (AS FAR AS WE KNOW) ONE GROUP IN ENGLAND, AND THAT WAS IN NORWICH. THEY WERE EVENTUALLY SUPPRESSED BY THE ROMAN CHURCH.

The plague resulted in a severe labor shortage, upsetting the rigidly hierarchical feudal system. When the king imposed a head tax to finance the "Hundred Year War" with France, the country erupted. In 1381, when Julian was 39, the Peasants' Revolt swept through England. It was centered mostly in London and Norwich, and came very close to totally overturning the country's feudal system.

Leading the battle against the rebelling peasants in Norfolk County was Bishop Henry Despenser, who was known as "the fighting bishop." He is probably the one who enclosed Julian in her anchorhold. A few years later, Despenser led a disastrous "crusade" into Flanders, just across the English Channel, further draining the country of healthy young men and money.

The Roman Catholic Church, the only church in Western Europe at that time, had sunk into moral and political chaos. During Julian's life, there were two popes (and for a while, three) hurling invective at each other. The church preached a vindictive God who set moral and spiritual laws that ordinary folk couldn't possibly understand, much less follow, and who then rained cataclysm on their confused heads when they "sinned." Julian and her family would have heard sermons in their church telling them that the plagues (and all the other tragedies) were God's punishment for sin. Ordinary folk, who couldn't afford the cost of having priests pray for them for years after their death, had little hope of a happy life hereafter.

At the same time, the first stirrings of the Protestant Reformation were beginning. John Wycliffe (sometimes call the "morning star of the Reformation") and his Lollard followers were challenging many of the key teachings of the church. The Lollards were particularly active in the area around Norwich, and the first burnings of Norfolk heretics began during Julian's lifetime. Some have wondered if Julian was a Lollard, though I think this is unlikely. But some of the things she writes in her book seem to reflect Lollard thinking. She certainly would have been aware of this movement.

In that desperately chaotic and terrible time, Julian wrote about her experience of a God who was totally different from what the church was preaching. We wonder how she managed not to be burned at the stake herself. Her ideas are radical, even by today's standards. Yet she insisted (and I believe her) that she was a faithful daughter of the church.

Julian writes out of a 14th-century pietism that focused very strongly on the pain and horror of the crucifixion of Jesus. Her visions were of the bleeding, suffering Christ. Even though I have skipped over much of that graphic material in my abridging of her manuscript, you may still find parts of the book a bit "off-putting." It is hard, in our sanitized culture, not to feel that Julian had a bit of an obsession with gore. Her 14th-century readers would not have shared that discomfort.

Others have complained that Julian seems to be going around in circles during the first part of her book. That is my impression also. Much of that has been removed in the pages that follow, but it was impossible to remove the circular arguments entirely and still be faithful to who she was and what she said.

The most significant (and also the longest) chapter in Julian's book is 51. Here she expands on the vision of the Lord and the Servant. It is from this that she develops her theology of a "mothering God" and of "our mother Jesus."

Some people feel hesitant or uncomfortable when they find themselves disagreeing with Julian. But she was a human being and subject to error just as you and I are. Even though I have found Julian's writing to be of immeasurable spiritual benefit, there are a number of places where I disagree with her. I think most thoughtful readers will have that experience. However, I think you'll find that

there are also many "pearls of great price" in her visions that are well worth digging for.

I host an online discussion group called *Julian's Cell*, which you can join by going to www.joinhands.com and following your nose to *Ralph's Resource Barrel*. There you can discuss the places you find troublesome or unclear, and read how the rest of us struggle with those issues.

It is impossible to summarize Julian's book in a few paragraphs, but listing what I think are a few key thoughts, may give you a helpful overview of her thinking.

Julian writes of a God who can only be described by one word. Love. Because God is only love and nothing else, God can't be angry. It is not that God forgives sins – it's that we live in a state of forgiveness. Always. More than that, Julian says it is against human nature to sin. For Julian, the Christian journey is really the discovery of our own authentic selves.

Julian's vision came from a God who yearns to be reunited with us. The word she uses is "oned." We are not complete until we have been "oned" with God, and she strongly implies that God is *not* complete until we have been reunited. We have the freedom to do all sorts of awful things, but God doesn't stop yearning to be reunited with us. Ever.

Julian probably read some of the writings by Augustine of Hippo. She would have been aware of Augustine's famous saying, "You have made us for Yourself, O God, and our hearts are restless till they rest in You." Writer Gerald Serafin was inspired by Julian to extend that thought: "Dare I add, O my God, that Your Heart is restless until it rests in me?"

As she struggles to find a way to describe this God who loves us so completely, Julian speaks of a "mothering" God, who yearns constantly for our welfare – who wants nothing more than to hold us

close as a mother holds her child. This mothering God looks on our sins "with pity, not with blame."

Julian is not saying that God is female. She also talks of God as "father." But God is "no person" she says, so such discussions about God's gender are really not helpful.

God's motherly nature is expressed through Christ. Julian speaks of "Christ our mother," who feeds us as a mother holds her child to her breast. Our mothering Christ feeds us in this way through the Eucharist or communion.

You have probably heard Julian's most quoted phrase: "All shall be well, and all shall be well, and all manner of thing shall be well." But you won't fully understand what she means by that evocative sentence until you have read more of her book.

My condensed paraphrase of Julian's *Revelations of Divine Love* will, I hope, lead you to find the full text of her writing, so that you may more fully explore the work of this spiritual giant who reaches across the centuries to speak a word of gentle, motherly love, to our troubled time.

Julian's Prayer

God of goodness
give me yourself.
You are enough to me.
I can ask for nothing less,
for then I would not be worshipping you.
And if I ask for anything less,
I will always be left wanting.
Only in you
do I have everything!

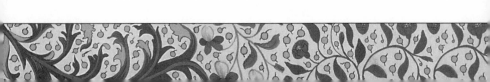

The Essence of Julian

This is a vision of love that Jesus Christ, who is our endless joy, gave to me.

These visions came to me, a simple and poorly educated woman, on May 8, 1373. But before that, I asked God for three gifts.

I was sure I already had a fairly good understanding of Jesus' death, but I wanted to learn – to feel much more deeply. I wanted to be like Mary Magdalene and the others who stood at the foot of the cross and watched Jesus die. So, as my first gift, I wanted to see the crucifixion through a vision, so that I might experience, deeply and fully, the pain Jesus suffered.

I don't know where the request for the second gift came from. But I found myself wanting to be so sick that those around me would think I was dying, and even give me the last rites of the church. I wanted to feel all the emotional and physical pain that goes with dying. This would help me overcome my fear of death so that I might live more fully and enter more deeply into the experience when it comes.

As for the third wish, I wanted God to remove my hard shell of indifference by giving me three sensitivities. The first one would help me be genuinely sorry for any wrong things I had done. The second was to respond naturally and helpfully to those who are sick or poor or dying. Thirdly, I asked that it would become a natural thing, a habit, to want to know more of God.

I soon forgot about the first two gifts, but the last one, the desire to be more intimate with God, never left me.

❧ CHAPTER 2*

*CHAPTER 1 IS OMITTED BECAUSE IT SIMPLY LISTS THE VARIOUS CHAPTERS.

When I was 30 and a half years old, God sent me an illness, in which I lay for three days and three nights. I thought I was dying and so did those around me. The priest came and gave me the last rites of the church.

I didn't want to die, not because there was anything in particular that I wanted to live for. Nor was I afraid of the pain of dying. I trusted God. But I wanted to live longer so that I could learn more about the love of God. Nevertheless, I said to myself, whatever is God's will is my will.

The next day my priest came and brought me a crucifix. "Here is the image of your Savior," he said gently. "Look on it. It will comfort you." By this time, every breath was painful, and I felt as if my whole body was dying, first the lower part, then the upper part. Everything became dark, except for a light around the crucifix.

Suddenly, all the pain was gone. I was convinced this was God's doing.

Then it occurred to me that I ought to ask again that I might have my whole body feel the pain and agony of Christ's crucifixion. I wanted his pains to be my pains, so that I would long for God. It seemed to me I should have those wounds, or sensitivities, so that I might develop compassion for the pain Jesus suffered. I wanted to suffer with Jesus, who became a human being because of God's love for all of us.

❧ CHAPTER 3

In my vision, as I gazed at the crucifix, I saw the red blood flowing out from under the crown of thorns on Christ's head. It was hot, running freely – a stream of blood, just as it must have been when they crucified Christ.

As I looked on the bleeding figure of Christ, suddenly the beauty of the Trinity filled my heart – God, Christ, the Holy Spirit.

> The Trinity is God,
> God is the Trinity.
> The Trinity is our maker and keeper.
> The Trinity is our everlasting lover –
> everlasting joy and happiness
> through our Lord Jesus Christ.

*"Benedicte Domine!"** I said. I was astonished that Christ, who is so great and wonderful and holy, would care about me, a sinful woman. Then I realized that Jesus wanted to comfort me and reassure me, before I would be tempted by devils trying to snare my soul as I was dying.

Then God gave me a vision of our blessed Mary, Jesus' mother. I saw her as she was, little more than a child, when she conceived. I saw the truth, the beauty and wisdom in her soul, which made it possible for her to say to the angel Gabriel, "Here I am, God's servant."

🌾 CHAPTER 4

* THIS EXCLAMATION IS NOT GOOD, GRAMMATICAL LATIN, BUT IT WAS A POPULAR EXPRESSION IN USE AT THE TIME.

As I was seeing the vision of Christ's bleeding head, he gave me a spiritual insight into his comforting love.

Christ is everything we need –
He is our clothing,
wrapping us in love.
Christ embraces us,
shelters us,
surrounds us
with his tender love.
Christ will never desert us!

And then Christ showed me a tiny, round thing. It was about the size of a hazelnut, which I held in the palm of my hand. And I wondered, "What might this be? How can this last? It is so tiny, it could just fade into nothing!"

This is the answer that came to me.

"In this small thing is all of creation!
It lasts
and it always will last
because God loves it.
In this way
all creation lasts
because
God made it,
God cares for it,
God loves it."

Out of this I learned that God wants to be known. We can find our true rest in God, not in the things around us.

> God of goodness
> give me yourself.
> You are enough to me.
> I can ask for nothing less,
> for then I would not be worshipping you.
> And if I ask for anything less,
> I will always be left wanting.
> Only in you
> do I have everything!*

CHAPTER 5

* THIS PASSAGE IS KNOWN AS "JULIAN'S PRAYER" AND IS OFTEN USED BY STUDY GROUPS OR IN SERVICES OF WORSHIP.

This vision was given to teach our souls to hold on tight to the goodness of God. God is delighted when we pray directly, not asking someone else to pray for us.

We pray to God –
to God in human flesh,
through God's precious blood,
and Holy Passion.
We pray to
Jesus' sweet mother, Mary,
to all the special saints
and blessed company of heaven.
All draw their power from God.

The goodness of God comes down to us in our most basic needs. It gives life to our souls, and helps us grow in grace and virtue.

We humans walk upright. We eat food which goes into our body. Then in time we have a bowel movement, after which our body is closed up like a well-made purse. It is God that makes this happen – even this lowly, basic bodily function.

God made us and loves us, even in our humblest needs, because we are created in God's image.

For as the body is clad in clothes
and the flesh is covered by skin
and the bones in the flesh
and the heart in the body;
so are we,
soul and body,
enclosed in the goodness of God.

It is part of our human nature to desire God, and it is part of God's nature to desire us. We can never stop yearning for God until we are possessed by God in the fullness of love.

❧ CHAPTER 6

During the time that I saw this vision of Christ on the cross, the great drops of blood, like pellets, fell down from under the garland of thorns. They were brownish red, but as they spread out, they turned bright red. When the drops came to his eyebrows, they vanished.

There was so much blood, running like the drops of water that fall from the roof after a great shower of rain. They fell so thick that no one could count them. As they spread over his forehead, I noticed that they were all rounded like the scales of a herring.*

> This vision was
> living and vivid,
> hideous and dreadful,
> sweet and lovely.

I was so encouraged when I realized that our God, who is so reverent and dreadful, is also friendly and open. This filled me with delight and confidence.

To make sure that I understood this, God gave me an example. I saw a vision of a mighty king or a very great lord, who was warm and kind to a very poor, very lowly servant. This vision was full of warmth and kindness.**

I thought to myself, "This is far more wonderful than if that royal person had given me many gifts." I realized this example was shown to me so that I would know that we could almost forget our own

---

* WE MAY FIND JULIAN'S GRAPHIC DESCRIPTIONS OF THE CRUCIFIXION UPSETTING – PERHAPS EVEN REVOLTING. BUT SUCH LANGUAGE WAS A NORMAL PART OF MEDIEVAL SPIRITUALITY. IT MAY HAVE BEEN EASIER FOR 14TH-CENTURY PEOPLE TO MEDITATE ON CHRIST'S SUFFERING AND DEATH, BECAUSE, IN A TIME WHEN THERE WERE NO HOSPITALS OR FUNERAL HOMES, SUFFERING AND DEATH WERE PART OF EVERYDAY REALITY.

** THE PARABLE OF THE LORD AND THE SERVANT IS FULLY DEVELOPED IN CHAPTER 51, WHERE IT BECOMES THE FOUNDATION OF JULIAN'S UNDERSTANDING OF A MOTHERING GOD.

miserable lives, because the kind lord makes life so joyful.

That is the way it is with Jesus and ourselves.

He is strong and exalted
noble and worthy
lowly and meek
friendly and courteous.
God wants us to
believe and trust,
enjoy and delight,
comfort
and cheer ourselves.

None of us can know this wonderful familiarity unless it is shown to us as God's gift. When we have been shown this, and the vision fades away, then we keep it alive and fresh through faith, by the grace of the Holy Spirit.

❧ CHAPTER 7

As long as I was seeing this vision, I couldn't stop saying, "Bless the Lord!" For I realized that God made all things for love, and by that same love all things are preserved and protected, and always shall be. The reason it all seemed to be so small, so little, was that I saw it in the presence of God.

> God is the maker of all things.
> God is everything that is good,
> and the goodness,
> which is there in all things,
> is God.

As I meditated on these things, I felt a profound love for all my fellow Christians. I hoped they would be able to see the beauty and truth of these visions, because I am sure they were intended for everyone.

During this time I expected to die, which was a surprise to me. And I felt sad because my visions were clearly intended for the living. I realized that everything that I said about myself applies to everyone – to all my fellow Christians.

So please, don't think about me. I am not important. Think about the kind, loving God who out of generous care for us, showed us this endless goodness. It is God's desire that you accept it with great joy and delight.

❧ CHAPTER 8

L et me be clear about this. I am not good or holy because I had these visions. Goodness and holiness come only as we love God more. If you love God more, then you will gain more than I.

I'm sure there are many who have never had great insights or visions, but only the ordinary teaching of the Church. They love God more than I do.

> For God is all that is good,
> and God made all that is made,
> and God loves every part of it.
> If you love all people
> because of God's love,
> then you love each created thing,
> because you love the creator.
> For God is in every person,
> and every person is in God.
> If you love in this way,
> you love all.

I am talking about those who will be saved, because that is all God showed me at this time.* I hold as true those things which my church preaches and teaches. I have never intended nor accepted anything which might be otherwise. It is my intention that as I meditate on my visions, I listen only for God's meaning.

❧ CHAPTER 9

---

* THE PHRASE "THOSE WHO WILL BE SAVED" OCCURS FREQUENTLY IN JULIAN'S BOOK. THERE IS SOME DEBATE ABOUT WHETHER JULIAN WAS A UNIVERSALIST – DID SHE BELIEVE THAT, IN GOD'S TIME, ALL HUMANITY WOULD BE SAVED? OR WOULD SOME GO TO ETERNAL HELL? THE QUESTION IS UNANSWERABLE, BECAUSE QUOTES FROM HER BOOK CAN BE FOUND TO SUPPORT EITHER POSITION. FOR WHAT IT'S WORTH, I THINK JULIAN BELIEVED IN UNIVERSAL SALVATION.

Then I looked again into the face of Christ on the cross.

> I saw scorn
> and spitting,
> and insults
> and beatings.

I saw all this dimly, fearfully. I wanted better light to see more clearly, but then I realized that if God wants us to see more, God will show us more.

> And so I saw God,
> I searched for God.
> I found God.
> I lost God.

That will be the usual way in which we experience God throughout our lives.

Once, as I was meditating, I found myself imagining what it would be like in the ocean. I could see the seaweed and the gravel and the moss. Then I realized that if a man or a woman were there, down in the sea, they would be safe in body and soul, and no harm would come to them.

If God protects us even in the deep, cold sea, then surely we are fully loved always because we are made in God's image. Then we humans fall so far, so painfully, because of our sin, that there is no way to restore us to life except through the help of the one who created us. God, who created us out of love, wants to restore us to the same joy – or even more.

It is God's will that we receive three gifts as the reward for our seeking. The first is the gift of diligence – that we work joyfully and

happily to live our faith, without a lot of hand-wringing or depression over our failures.

The second gift is patience to wait for God, without grumbling and fussing when it seems we are not moving fast enough.

The third gift is trust – confidence that God will come to us, suddenly and wonderfully.

We are taught in church that we are created in the image of the blessed Trinity. We also know that humans fell so deeply and so terribly into sin that there was only one way to restore us to wholeness. The one who created us out of love by that same love wants to restore us to that joyful wholeness and even more.

CHAPTER 10

Then I saw God focused in a point – the still center of creation. Through that vision, I realized that if God is the center of all things, then God is present in all things. In other words, God does everything that is done.

I began to be afraid as I thought about this. Because if God is present in all things, does that mean that God is part of our sin? I saw that God does everything, no matter how insignificant. Nothing happens by chance, but everything happens through God's far-sighted wisdom. It may seem to us that things happen through pure, random chance, but that's because of our blindness – our lack of foresight.

So I had to recognize that everything that is done, is done well. God does everything, because God is the center of everything.

And God does not sin.

So therefore sin is not something we do. Then I realized that in all my visions, sin was not shown to me.

We humans think of some things as good, and other things as bad. God doesn't see them that way, because everything in nature is God's doing. God has made everything totally good. And everything that is done, is done by God.

God revealed all this to me in a most wonderful way.

"See!
I am God.
See!
I am in everything.
See!
I do all things.
See!
I never take my hands off my work,
and I never shall.

See!
I lead each thing
toward the purpose I ordained for it,
without beginning,
and with the same strength, wisdom, and love
that brought it into being.
How can anything be amiss?"

Then I found I could do nothing but agree, and this with deep reverence. I could do nothing except simply enjoy God.

CHAPTER 11*

* CHAPTER 12 WAS OMITTED BECAUSE THE CONTENTS SEEMED LESS RELEVANT THAN THEY WOULD HAVE BEEN WHEN JULIAN PENNED THESE WORDS 600 YEARS AGO.

I heard no words when I saw the deep pain and copious blood of Christ's crucifixion. But later, when I was still thinking about Christ's passion, God formed this thought in my soul: "This is how the Devil is overcome!" While I realized that the fiend keeps scheming and plotting ways to trap us, God allows him to work but always puts him to shame. The Devil's power is all in God's hands.

But God doesn't show anger against the fiend. With power and justice, God turns all the Devil's works to the benefit of all who will be saved.

When I saw this I laughed out loud. Those around me laughed out loud too. I wished that all my fellow Christians could have seen what I saw, and laughed with me. I didn't actually see Christ laugh, but it was the vision he showed me that made me laugh. So I realized that we may laugh and rejoice in God, because it is through such laughter that the Devil is overcome.

❧ CHAPTER 13

Then our good Lord said to me, "Thank you for the work you did for me in your youth." As I meditated on this, I saw how all God's friends had been invited to a great feast. But God didn't sit on a throne or at the head table, waiting for people to come and offer worship. God walked around the banquet hall, talking and smiling and showing love and grace to everyone who was there. The whole place seemed filled with marvelous melody and endless love.

Then I understood the joy that everyone will have in heaven – everyone who has ever served God in some way. They will be thanked by God the moment they are delivered from the pain of earthly life. All who are in heaven will see this, because God will make their service known to everyone. And this joy will last forever.

I saw how the life story of everyone will be told in heaven, even if they willingly served God for only one day of their lives. The more we see of this graciousness, the more we will want to serve God with our lives.

❧ CHAPTER 14

I saw that God took great, spiritual delight in my soul. Because of that, I felt so strong, so spiritual that I was completely at ease.

My laughter and delight only lasted for a short while. Then I found myself changed. I felt abandoned. Depressed. Weary of life. But after a while, God gave me comfort again, so that I felt no fear, no depression, no physical or spiritual pain.

Then again the depression. Then the delight. First one then the other – I suppose about 20 times.

When I was feeling joy, I could have said with Saint Paul, "Nothing can separate me from the love of Christ." When I was depressed I could have said with Saint Peter, "Lord, save me. I am dying."

I knew joy one moment and pain the next. I was given this experience for a reason. Sometimes God leaves us on our own for the good of our soul. Sometimes God brings us joy and sometimes pain, but both are one love. Joy lasts, but pain is passing. God doesn't want us to feel pain, but wants us to pass right by that pain and live in God's endless love.

❦ CHAPTER 15

Then Christ showed me a part of his passion near his death. I saw his sweet face dry and bloodless – deadly pale. Then I saw the painful change, when he turned brown and black, and his complexion shriveled into the image of death.

I felt a bitter, cold, dry wind, which dried up Christ's flesh. The long agony, the torture, seemed to me as if it went on for many days. His tender body became so dry – so discolored, so deathly, so pitiful – that he might have been dead for a week. This was the greatest and the last pain of his passion – when his flesh dried up.

❦ CHAPTER 16

37 THE ESSENCE OF JULIAN

In this prolonged drying, I remembered the words of Christ on the cross. "I thirst!" I saw a double thirst, the thirst of his body and the thirst of his spirit.

I saw his body ripped to pieces like a cloth. His skin was covered with fine wrinkles, the color of leather, or like a dry piece of wood.

This vision of Christ's pains filled me again with pain. Then I thought, "I hardly knew what kind of pain it was I had asked for." Like a wretch, I regretted it. If I had known how terrible this would be, I wouldn't have asked for it. It seemed to me as if the pain I felt was worse than the pain of dying.

"Is any pain like this?" I wondered. Then the answer came to me. "Hell is another kind of pain – the pain of despair. But of all the pains that lead to salvation, this is the deepest pain – to see the one you love suffer."

<blockquote>
How might any pain be more piercing
than to see such suffering
in the one who is
my life,
my happiness,
my joy?
</blockquote>

I loved Christ so much that there was no greater pain, no deeper sorrow, than what I felt as I saw him suffer and die.

❧ CHAPTER 17

Here I saw some of the compassion of his mother, Mary. They were so united in their love that the greatness of her love caused the depth of her pain. All of his disciples who loved him so deeply felt more pain when they watched him die than they did when they themselves died.

In this, I saw a fundamental unity between Christ and all creation – between Christ and us. All creatures that were able to feel pain, felt it. Even the sky and the earth fractured when Jesus died on the cross.

Those who were his friends suffered pain because of their love for him. And those who didn't know him suffered because all creation crumbled. Even those who didn't know Christ, suffered when he died.

In this way our Lord was brought to nothing for us, and we are brought to nothing for him.

❦ CHAPTER 18

As I said before, if I had known what kind of pain this would be, I wouldn't have prayed for it. My weak body would have refused it. My soul did not agree to this. But God assigns no blame for this grumbling that came from my body. This reluctance and my soul making deliberate choices are opposite things, and I felt them both at the same time. These are two parts of who we are, the outward and the inner parts of ourselves.

The outward part is our physical body, which often gives us pain and sorrow. That will continue all our lives. It was this physical part, my body, that was now giving me trouble.

But inside myself, my soul was filled with peace and love. It was through this part of me that I very deliberately chose Jesus to be my heaven.

This is how I realized that my inner self, my soul, is in charge of my body, and is always struggling, working to be united with our Lord Jesus. This inner self draws my outer self, my physical being, until by grace both will be united through the power of Christ.

❧ CHAPTER 19

I saw our Lord Jesus lingering for a long time on the cross. That was because the union of God and humanity in this one person made it possible for him to suffer more than anyone – not just more than another individual, but more than all the people from the beginning of time could have suffered together.

Jesus, the highest, most honorable, was completely humiliated and utterly despised. We can't even imagine his suffering until we understand who it was that suffered in this way.

Jesus suffered for everyone's sins. He saw and grieved for all human sorrow, loneliness, and pain. I saw that the love he has for our souls was so strong, he freely chose that great suffering – chose it with great joy. The soul that understands this, when it is touched by grace, will really see how the pain of Christ's passion was greater than all pains. It was greater than any pains we may suffer for God's sake – pains which will be turned into endless joy by the power of Christ's passion.

CHAPTER 20

As I looked on the suffering Christ, I waited for the moment of death, which I thought would come at any moment. Yet, as I looked at the cross, his appearance changed to joy! Seeing that, I also felt joyful and happy. Then he cheerfully put some words into my mind – "Where is all your grief and pain now?"

In my joy, I understood that our Lord means that in the struggles of our life we are, in a sense, on the cross with him. If, of our own free will, we stay on that cross – if we accept the suffering that goes with living out our faith (which we can only do with his help and grace) – then Christ will make us heirs with him in his eternal joy.

Through this little pain, which we suffer here on earth, we will have a deep and eternal knowledge of God – something we could never have without it.

❧ CHAPTER 21

Then our good Lord Jesus Christ asked, "Are you satisfied by the way I suffered for you?" I said, "Oh, yes, Lord. Yes!"

"If you are satisfied, then I am satisfied," said Jesus. "It is a deep and endless joy to me that I was able to suffer for you. Still, if I could suffer more for you, I would gladly do it."

So I understood that Jesus counted his death as nothing in comparison with his love for us. He is ready, every day, to do it again. He could make new heavens and new earths in an instant and without effort. But the greatest gift God can give to us is to die for us, over and over again.

This, then, was his meaning. "How could there be anything I wouldn't do for you?" This love was without a beginning, and there will be no end. Here I saw that Christ's joy is complete, because his great deed could not have been done more wonderfully, or in any other way.

❦ CHAPTER 22

I t is God's purpose
that we be delighted –
that we enjoy the gift of salvation –
that we be comforted
and strengthened through grace.
We are God's happiness and delight.
And God is our happiness and delight!

This contemplation of Christ's passion brought to mind the nature of a cheerful giver. A cheerful giver is never concerned about the cost and trouble that went into the gift. The giver is only concerned about the joy of the person who will receive it. If the gift is received with gladness, then the giver is rewarded by that delight.

The gift we receive is to become God's crown and everlasting joy.

❧ CHAPTER 23

Then, his face full of joy, our Lord looked into his wounded side. He led me into his wound and showed me a lovely place, large enough for all humanity to rest in peace and love.

Then I remembered the way his wound shed blood and water. He showed me his great heart, broken in two. And I was profoundly aware that this was because of the endless love that was without beginning and will be without end.

For my own deeper understanding, I heard the words, "See how I love you! If you pray and ask for anything that is pleasing to me, I will grant it. For I delight in your holiness and in the way you find your joy in me."

God said those words to make us glad and joyful. "See how I love you!"

❧ CHAPTER 24

In my vision, Jesus looked down toward his right, to the place where our Lady Mary stood during his crucifixion. He said to me, "Yes, I know you want to see my wonderful mother. I want you to see how I love her, so that you might celebrate with me the love that I have in her and she in me."

Those words were addressed to me, but they were meant for all humanity, as if it were just one person. "Would you like to see how you are loved? It was for love of you that I made my mother high and noble." Jesus wanted us to know that all those that love him should also love her. For if you love someone in a special way above everything else, then you want everyone to love and find pleasure in that special person.

Our Lord showed me no other individual, except his mother Mary. And I saw her on three occasions. When she conceived, when she stood at the foot of the cross, and where she is now with God, in delight, honor, and joy.

&❦ CHAPTER 25

Again, our Lord showed himself to me, this time more glorious than I had seen him before. I learned that our soul will never find rest until it comes to the fullness of his joy.

So our Lord said, again and again:

"I am the one.
I am the one.
I am the one most honored.
I am the one you love.
I am the one you enjoy.
I am the one you serve.
I am the one you long for.
I am the one you desire.
I am the one you yearn for.
I am the one who is everything.
I am the one whom the holy church preaches and teaches.
I am the one who showed myself to you."

There were so many words, I couldn't understand them all. But the joy I had in listening to those words went far beyond anything I could think or desire. I won't try to explain them, but, as the grace of God gives you love and understanding, you will know what God means.

❧ CHAPTER 26

As I reflected on the longing I had to be one with Jesus, I saw that nothing was keeping me back except sin. This, of course, is true of all of us. It seemed to me that if there were no sin, then we would be whole – spiritually healthy, just like Jesus.

Since God can foresee everything that will happen, I often wondered why sin had not been stopped, right at the beginning. Then everything would be just fine.

Jesus answered me with these words:

> "Sin is inevitable.
> But all shall be well,
> and all shall be well,
> and all manner of thing shall be well."

In that naked word "sin," our Lord brought to my mind everything that isn't good – his death and suffering – and the pain and suffering of all God's creatures.

But I didn't see sin. Sin has no substance – no reality of its own. We don't recognize sin except by the pain it causes. In this our Lord comforts us, readily and gladly, and shows us that, indeed,

> Sin is the cause of all this pain.
> But all shall be well,
> and all shall be well
> and all manner of thing shall be well.

Those words were spoken gently and carried no blame for me or anyone else. Through all this I saw a deep mystery hidden in God, which we will all understand someday in heaven. Then we will know why God allowed sin to be part of this world. That knowledge will give us endless joy.

❧ CHAPTER 27

I saw how Christ has compassion on us because of our sin. Just as, before this, I was filled with compassion for Christ on the cross, so now I was filled with compassion for my fellow Christians who always seem to be drawn into sin. God loves us very dearly, even though the church will be shaken with trouble and sorrow the way we shake a cloth in the wind.

Then Christ says, "I will purge you of your selfishness and your pride, and then I will gather you to myself to make you kind, gentle, and holy, by joining you to myself. I want to be the soil in which you grow."

I realized then that each time we have compassion and love for our fellow Christians, it is Christ in us. And in his great gentleness, Christ puts away all our blame and looks on us with pity and love, as if we were innocent children.

❧ CHAPTER 28

As I stood, shaking with grief and sorrow, I found myself saying words to Christ. "Oh, good Lord, how can all things be well? Look at all the great harm that sin has caused among your creatures!" I wanted a more clear explanation of all this.

So Christ answered very gently and kindly. He showed me that the sin of Adam was the worst thing that was ever done. But Christ's atonement more than made up for Adam's sin.

I understood that the Lord was showing me that since the greatest of sins had been made right, then he will set right all the lesser sins as well.

CHAPTER 29

Then I was given to understand two things. The first, which is about our Savior and how we can be saved, is open, and clear and enjoyable and generous.

All people of good will can understand this part. Even so, we must work at this, enjoying Christ just as he enjoys us. The more we accept this, the more progress we will make in our spiritual lives. We are given this gift – to learn and enjoy God.

The second is hidden from us – the part that is not necessary for our own salvation. This is God's private concern, which we should respect. In fact, if those who want to know and understand everything would just leave this second kind of understanding alone, they would be much happier and so would God.

Let us trust God, and be glad in everything!

❧ CHAPTER 30

O ur good Lord answered all my questions and doubts by saying very gently,

> "I may make all things well;
> I can make all things well;
> I will make all things well;
> and you will see for yourself,
> that all manner of thing shall be well."

With these comforting words, God wants us to be embraced in a sense of rest and peace. When that happens, Christ's spiritual thirst will be satisfied. But Christ is not finished with the suffering of the cross, because that same love-longing, that same thirst that he had then, will not be satisfied until the last soul has been made whole through becoming one with him.

God has pity and compassion on us, always longing to be one with us. But God's wisdom and love will not let the end come until the right time.

❧ CHAPTER 31

Our good Lord said to me, "Every kind of thing shall be well," and at another time I was told, "You'll see for yourself that every kind of thing will be well."

I learned two things from this. First, God wants us to know that it is not only the great, wonderful, and noble things that will be made well, but also the small things – ordinary people – everything will be made well. Nothing and nobody will be forgotten.

Second, there are so many evil things that happen – tragedies and atrocities. That's because we humans are so blind, so base, so stupid that we don't recognize the glorious wisdom of God.

So this is what I understand. There is a deed which God will do on the Last Day. We will never know what that deed is going to be until it is actually done. Through this great deed, God will make all things well. God made all things from nothing – the good and the bad – and in the end will make whole all those things which are now broken.

Here is my problem. My church teaches me that many people will be damned – those who have never accepted the Christian faith, and those who were Christians but who lived evil lives. All these will be eternally damned.

Given that, it seems impossible that everything would be made well, as I had learned in my vision. I didn't get any other explanation than this: "What is impossible for you is not impossible for me. I will make all things well."

We don't know what will happen until it has happened. God's word will be preserved in everything.

We simply trust God.

❧ CHAPTER 32

I wanted to have some sight of hell and purgatory. I wasn't trying to check on what the church teaches me. I just wanted to understand a little more.

But I was shown nothing of this. The visions I'd had showed me mostly good things, with very little mention of things that were evil.

I saw Christ's death on the cross in several of my visions, as I've told you already. I saw the pain of Mary, his mother, and of the various friends who were there at his crucifixion. But God showed me nothing about the Jews who, according to the church, crucified Christ.*

God wants us to pay attention to all that has been done – and to trust and to believe all that God will do. But we are not to spend time trying to figure out what God will do. Let's rejoice and be satisfied with what God reveals to us, and with what remains hidden.

The more we busy ourselves trying to figure out what God is going to do, the further we are from really knowing how we should live.

❧ CHAPTER 33

* IN JULIAN'S TIME, IT WAS SIMPLY ASSUMED THAT ALL JEWS WERE EVIL, AS WERE ALL MUSLIMS. JULIAN, A WOMAN OF HER TIME, SIMPLY REFLECTS THE PREJUDICE OF HER ERA.

God showed me two kinds of mysteries.

There is the great mystery, which will be hidden until the time when God shows it to us.

The second mystery is the one God showed me in my visions – the one that is there for all of us if we don't let our blindness and ignorance get in the way. Everything we need is there for us in the preaching and teaching of the church.

God has great delight in all women and men who accept this teaching.

For God is the church.
God is the foundation,
the substance,
the teaching,
and the teacher.
God is the purpose
and the reward,
for which every human soul searches.

All of this helps us in our struggle against sin. When I was shown that God does everything that is done, I did not see sin. I saw that all will be well. But when God did show me sin, even then I saw that all will be well.

❧ CHAPTER 34

I came to God to ask about a certain person that I loved. What will be her future? Will she continue with the good life that she has begun?

Then, through my reason, God provided me with an answer. Focus on all the goodness of God. It is better to know God in everything than to take delight in one special thing. In other words, I shouldn't be glad because of one good thing that happens or be sad because something bad happens.

God has told us. "All will be well!"

> Everything God does
> is good.
> Everything God tolerates
> is honorable.

In those two statements, we can understand good and evil. I'm not saying that evil is honorable. But God's toleration of evil is a good and necessary thing, through which God's loving kindness will be known forever.

❧ CHAPTER 35

God showed me that a deed will be done. It will be wonderful and generous, even though we do nothing but sin.

The great love that God has for us shows that we may rejoice in all that we are shown. We can find deep comfort in it, and give God endless thanks for it.

It's as if God touches us tenderly and says, "Attend to me, my precious child. I am enough for you. Rejoice in your Savior and in your salvation."

❧ CHAPTER 36

God brought it to my mind that I would sin. But I was enjoying the holy presence so much that I didn't really think about what I had just been shown.

So God waited, very gently and patiently. Eventually, I learned that this was a teaching that didn't just apply to me – it applied to everyone. Everyone will sin.

In this teaching, I felt such love and reassurance – for myself and for all my fellow Christians. What could possibly help me love them more than to see how God loves them as if they were all one soul.

For in every soul there is a higher will that never agrees to sin. And there is a savage will in the lower part of our humanity that can never want to do anything except evil. Even so, we all stand as one in God's sight, and we are loved now, right where we are, as much as we will be loved when we come into God's presence.

❧ CHAPTER 37

God showed me that we should not feel guilt because of our sin. Just as every sin brings its own suffering, so when we sin, we also earn a blessing.

The greater the sin, the more painful is the punishment, but in heaven we will be rewarded for our victories over those sins – a reward that will reflect the pain of the punishment we suffered for them.

Every one of us is so precious to God, and our place in heaven will be so honorable, that God never allows us to sin in such a way that we could not come there. God pointed to saints such as King David, Mary Magdalene, Peter, Paul, Thomas of India, John of Beverly, and many others. We know about their sins, but now everything is turned into glory for them.

❧ CHAPTER 38

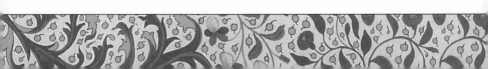

Sin is the sharpest lash that can hurt us. This lash repeatedly thrashes us painfully, so that we begin to think we are not fit for anything except hell. Then the Holy Spirit helps us turn this bitterness into a hope of God's mercy. Then the wounds begin to heal and our soul feels new life. That leads us to confess our sins, candidly, openly, and with genuine regret and desire for forgiveness.

Our good Lord protects us when we feel completely alone and abandoned, especially when we think we deserve to be this way. Then God comes to us with grace and compassion, so that we are delivered from our sin and our pain.

> We repent and are made clean;
> we feel compassion and are made ready;
> we yearn for God and become worthy.

Every sinful soul needs to be healed in this way. Our emotional wounds are not seen by God as scars, but as marks of honor. Our sin brings us pain and grief, but God responds with love, not blame.

All our guilt will be turned into honor and joy because God doesn't want us to despair. Even though we keep messing up our lives, God loves us anyway.

Peace and love are always working inside us, even though we are not always living this peace and love. God is the source of our whole life in love, and defends us against our enemies who are very cruel and determined.

❦ CHAPTER 39

Often we see ourselves as basically foul and we assume that God must be angry at us.

But God comes to us and says, "Dear child, I'm glad you have come to me with all your struggles. I have always been with you, and I have always loved you. In the joy of that love, we can become one."

Now if any of us might think, well, if God is like that, then it would be good to do a lot of sinning so that I could have even greater rewards in the end. Or we might just think that sin isn't really important.

Don't let yourself think that way! That is the Devil leading you astray!

The love that touches us and gives us strength is the same love that teaches us that we must hate sin and struggle against it. The reality is that the pain which sin creates in us is worse than all the pain of hell, purgatory, death, and all the rest. I saw no more cruel hell than sin.

God is willing and powerful and wants to save us. Christ himself is the source of all the laws of Christian people. He taught us to do good in response to evil. Christ himself is this love, and wants us to be like him in everlasting love of ourselves and of our fellow Christians. Christ doesn't withdraw his love from us when we sin and he doesn't want us to withdraw our love from our fellow Christians when they sin.

Let us hate sin
the way God hates it,
and love the human soul
the way God loves it.

❦ CHAPTER 40

Then our Lord taught me about prayer.

If we pray without trust in God, not fully convinced that God hears us, we may feel nothing at all, and at the end of the prayer we are as dry and hopeless as before. I know. I've experienced this loneliness myself.

God says to us, "I am the foundation of your prayer. It is my will that you should have what you ask. So first I make you want it and then I make you ask for it. So how could it be that you don't have what you ask for?"

Our prayer makes God happy. God says to us, "Pray with enthusiasm, even if it seems there is little substance to your prayer. It is good for you, even if you don't feel the benefits. Pray wholeheartedly, even if it feels as if you can't or don't want to pray because you feel dry and barren, or sick and weak. It is in those painful times that your prayer pleases me the most, even if it feels mechanical and without passion."

God wants us to be praying constantly – actually living our prayers. God accepts our prayer and our work, whether we feel enthusiastic about them or not.

Give thanks when you pray. Thanksgiving is the deep, inner certainty that moves us to an inward sense of awe and wonder at God's gifts. Sometimes we are so grateful that we simply shout it, "Thank you, Lord!"

Sometimes our hearts are dry and unfeeling. Then we need to use our reason and our knowledge of grace to make ourselves pray, imploring God to help us remember Christ's blessed passion and goodness.

Then the power of our Lord's word will enter your soul and you will be able to pray again with a strong sense of the blessings you have received. Then you will be able to rejoice and offer a genuine prayer of thanksgiving.

CHAPTER 41

God wants us to really understand prayer.

We need to understand from whom our prayer originates. "I am the source," God said to me, which means that all prayer comes from God. Secondly, the purpose of prayer is to unite our will with the will of God.

Thirdly, God wants us to know the result of our prayers – which is to be united, to be one with God in every way.

I don't think we would ask for mercy and grace unless mercy and grace were first shown to us. When we feel that we have prayed for a long time and our prayers haven't been answered, we need not feel depressed over it. I'm sure that God is telling us to wait for another time, or a different occasion, or more grace. We need to understand and trust God, and learn to live in that trust.

When, through grace, we have that kind of an understanding of God, then three things follow. The first is knowledge of the way we were created. The second is the wonderful way in which Christ died for us. And the third is the way all creation has been given to us, to serve us. And God cares for this creation out of love for us.

Then God says, "Look! See everything I did for you, even before you began to pray. And now you are here, and you can pray to me."

Prayer is a full understanding of all the joy that is promised to us. When we sense, when we can taste that joy, we naturally long for a true understanding of that love. Then, through grace, we begin to trust.

In all this we can completely overcome all our weakness – all our doubts and depression.

❦ CHAPTER 42

Prayer unites the soul with God. Even though our soul is always like God in nature and in essence, its actual condition, because of sin, might make it unlike God. So our prayer reminds us that the soul's will is God's will. Our conscience is healed as grace brings us back into union with God.

God teaches us to pray and to be confident that we will receive what we pray for. God encourages us to pray for what we should have. God looks at us with love, and wants us as partners.

God shows such pleasure and such delight when we pray in this way, almost as if we did this on our own.

The more our soul sees of God, the more we desire God, even though sometimes we are sliding away and unfit to be in God's holy presence. That is the very time for our soul to pray, to become more pliable, more fit to be with God.

Whenever we feel the need to pray, we know that the Lord God is right behind us, encouraging our prayer. And when we, by special grace, see God clearly, we then turn to follow. We are drawn forward by God's love.

And so by grace, and by our own humble prayer, we come to God in this life. We sense the touch of holiness and experience the presence through spiritual insights and generous feelings measured out to us as we grow and are able to bear them. This is done by the Holy Spirit until the day we die, still longing for love.

Then we will all come into our Lord's presence knowing ourselves clearly and possessing God fully. Then we will

see God truly,
touch God fully,
hear God spiritually
smell God delectably,
taste God sweetly.

Then we will see God face to face – fully and generously. Then we, the creatures that are made, will see the face of God our maker.

❧ CHAPTER 43

Truth sees God;
wisdom perceives God,
and from these two comes a third,
the holy, wondering delight in God,
which is love.
Wherever there is truth and wisdom, there we will find God.
For God is endless truth
and supreme wisdom,
a love that is uncreated.
We are created by God, with the same divine qualities as
God. And in our soul we do what we were created for.
We see God;
we think about God;
we love God.
Therefore, God rejoices in us
and we rejoice in God.

That we are of the same substance as God seems so impossible to us, because we can hardly see any worth in ourselves, especially in comparison with God. But this bright, clear truth and wisdom helps us know that God created us for love. And in that love, God protects us.

❦ CHAPTER 44

God judges us by the essence of our human nature. And God keeps our nature whole and safe forever.

Others judge us by what they see us do, which is sometimes kind and understanding, and sometimes hard and painful. When others are kind and understanding, that is God's justice. When other people's judgment is hard and painful, our good Lord takes that judgment and reforms it through mercy and grace and so brings it into justice.

In the light of that justice, I realized that we are sinners and sometimes deserve blame and anger. But I couldn't see anger or blame in God. I didn't understand this until I had the vision of the Lord and the Servant, which I will tell you about later.

The more we know and understand our own failings, the more our essential nature will yearn to be brought into fulfillment in God's endless joy and bliss. That is the reason God made us. The essence of our human nature is God's endless delight.

❧ CHAPTER 45

As human creatures, living in our bodies, we don't really know ourselves. But by faith we can learn who we really are.

When we truly and clearly know ourselves, then we will also know God.

We can learn to know ourselves more and more through the help of our highest human nature, which is aided by God's mercy and grace. But we will never completely know ourselves until that last moment when our lives come to an end.

As we grow to know ourselves, we will realize that we are all sinners. We do things we shouldn't do, and we leave undone things that we should be doing. And it seems to us that we really deserve God's anger.

But in my vision, I saw that God is never angry.

> God is goodness,
> truth, love, and peace.
> God is power,
> wisdom,
> love, and unity.

It is against the very nature of God to be angry. God is nothing but goodness! Our soul is united with God who is unchangeable goodness, so there can never be anger between us.

It is God's will that our simple souls should know and understand everything we are capable of understanding. As for the rest, God keeps it a secret out of love for us.

❧ CHAPTER 46

Our souls have two obligations: one is to marvel; the other is to accept the suffering that comes our way, and in both cases to find our joy in God.

God wants us to know that in a short time at the end of our lives we will know and understand everything.

I had been taught that God's mercy meant that when our sins are forgiven, God would no longer be angry. God's wrath would be the hardest thing for us to bear. But in my showings, I did not see God withdraw wrath. You can't withdraw something that was never there.

We humans are very changeable. We're weak and we fall easily into sin. We lose all our common sense and we slide down into turmoil, grief, and despair. We're blind. We don't see God. If we could see God continually, then we wouldn't get ourselves into such a mix-up.

This kind of vision simply can't be continuous in our lives. We are human and distracted by many things. We fall back into ourselves – into the fundamental sinfulness that is part of our nature.

We find ourselves deeply troubled, kicked around by conflicting emotions, feeling pain in our spirits and in our bodies. This seems to be our human experience.

❦ CHAPTER 47

Even so, the Holy Spirit, who is endless life, lives in our souls. The Spirit keeps us safe and secure, and brings us to a sense of peace. This is the merciful way in which our Good Lord constantly leads us.

It's we who get angry. Not God. We feel anger because we are quarrelsome and selfish. This comes to us because we are weak, or we lack wisdom, but it all originates with God.

> Our failing is awful;
> our falling is shameful;
> our dying is sorrowful.

In all this, the sweet eye of God's pity never looks away from us. The work of mercy never stops.

Mercy is that sense of love for the one who is in pain and it is an attribute of motherhood – of tender love.

Thinking about all this, I realized that the function of mercy is to quench our anger, not God's.

❧ CHAPTER 48

I shake my head in wonder at it all. In the vision that God showed to my soul, I saw that God can't forgive because God can't be angry! It's impossible!

Our life is completely rooted in love. We can't live without love. This is because we are united with God in love and God can never be angry with us. Anger and friendship are opposites. Wherever our Lord appears, peace is there. Anger has no place.

Our endless friendship, our home, our life, our very being – everything is rooted in God. It is God's endless goodness that protects us when we sin. That same endless goodness continually makes peace between ourselves and our own anger – our own perversity.

However, we can't be completely safe - completely at peace – until we are content with ourselves, with our fellow Christians, and with everything that God loves.

God is our peace. Whenever we are restless and insecure, God watches over us continually. When, by power and mercy we become gentle and kind, then we are completely safe, because our soul is at peace with God.

Our Lord takes all our mixed-up, contradictory emotions and sends them up to heaven where they are turned into beautiful and lasting glory.

So God is our steadfast foundation and our whole joy.

CHAPTER 49

In our mortal life, mercy and forgiveness are the virtues that lead us to grace. Still, we fall into many kinds of temptations – enough that those around us think we are spiritually dead. But in the sight of God, we are very much alive.

Even so, I found myself saying, "Good Lord, I can see that you are the essence of truth. I also know that we sin all the time, every day. We really are to blame for this. That is obvious to me, but at the same time, you don't seem to place this guilt on us. My church taught me that we are to blame for our sins – from the sins of the first human up to the present day. So this is why I am so surprised that you don't seem to lay any blame on me. You treat me as if I was as pure as an angel!"

Between those two opposites, anger and friendship, I couldn't find any rest. I was afraid that even with my wonderful visions, I would not really understand how God looks on our sin. I kept looking for clarity, but I felt more and more perplexed. "If it's true that we are sinners – to blame for all the evil that we do, then how is it, God, that I can't see this in my vision of you? I really need to know! How can I find any comfort? Who is going to teach me, if I can't see it in you?"

✤ CHAPTER 50

Seeing my confusion, God gave me a parable, about a Lord and a Servant, though at first I wasn't at all clear about what it meant.

I saw two people, who looked quite a lot like each other, actually.

The Lord sits comfortably, while nearby stands the servant. You can tell the Lord really loves this servant, and that the servant is ready to do anything the Lord asks.

So the Lord sends the servant on an errand. The servant not only goes, he dashes off as fast as he can, promptly falling into a deep and muddy ditch. He is badly injured. He groans and moans, but he can't get up. He can't see that the Lord is still near him. All the servant can feel is his own pain – all he can see is the mud at the bottom of the ditch.

Then I looked at the servant in the ditch to see if he had done something wrong. Was he to blame for his falling? I saw immediately that he got into this mess because he wanted so much to please his Lord. The Lord is standing by and loves the servant as much as ever, even though the servant is not aware of this.

Then the Lord speaks. "Poor fellow! He really got into a terrible mess and is badly hurt because he loved me and was trying to please me. I really must give him some reward that repays him for all this. Actually, I think I should do more than just repay him, or it would seem I'm not really grateful at all."

Even with all this, I was still really confused about what the parable was saying, and I still didn't understand why God doesn't blame us for sin, or why sin is necessary in the first place. Even 20 years after my visions, I still didn't really understand this parable.

Then God gave me an insight. "The truth is in the details. Pay attention to everything in the parable." So that's what I did. In my mind's eye, I looked at the parable again and again, focusing on every little thing – the color and style of the clothes they wore, how they stood or sat in relation to each other, the expression on their faces. Eventually I began to understand, at least a little.

In the parable, the Lord sits calmly and comfortably. That Lord represents God. The servant standing there is Adam. Adam stands for all humanity. In the sight of God, this Adam represents every one of us. This Adam is weak, injured, feeble. He doesn't know what is happening and turns away from the Lord, even though God praises Adam and affirms him. Adam somehow can't understand this, and is miserable and hurting because of his humanity. Adam can't see the Lord, and can't really see himself reflected in the loving face of God.

The place where the Lord sits is simple. He is in a desert, alone in the wilderness. His clothing is beautiful – blue as azure. His bronzed face is gentle and kind. His eyes are black and sparkled with love. The blueness stands for faithfulness, and his bronzed face and dark eyes signify God's holy purpose.

The Lord watches the servant constantly, especially when the servant falls into the ditch. This Lord is like God, whose loving gaze covers all the earth. God watches Adam fall and the gentle, loving gaze follows him right down into hell. God's love keeps Adam (in other words, all of us) from everlasting death.

In our life, we are blinded. We don't see the Father, our God. And I saw very clearly that even though we think of God as Father, this Father is not a human – not a man.

God created the human soul for a dwelling place. Of all creation, God loves our human soul the best. And when Adam fell into sorrow and pain, he couldn't offer his soul as a dwelling for God, and yet God would not create any other place in which to dwell. God would wait patiently until God's son, Jesus the Christ, rescued his soul by his terrifying and painful death.

Still I kept studying the parable in my mind's eye. I gradually began to see it in more detail. The servant was dressed very simply. Poorly. He was half-naked, with a dirty, white, sweat-stained smock that seemed ready to fall off, it was so worn.

Then the servant realized there was only one thing he could do for his Lord. He ran off quickly at the Lord's suggestion, to find a treasure in the earth. I wondered what that could possibly be. Then I saw that the servant became a gardener, who dug the earth and planted seeds, and watered them. When the garden had grown, the servant took the treasure, a delectable meal, to the Lord – all the sweet fruit of the garden, prepared carefully and with love. This image kept me puzzling, trying to find out what all this meant.

When things became a little clearer, I realized that the servant, Adam, is the Second Person of the Trinity. He is Adam, but he is also the Christ. When humanity (Adam) fell, God's Son fell. The original Adam fell from life into death, but Christ, the second Adam, fell into a woman's womb.

So in the wisdom and goodness of the servant who wants so much to please his master, we see Jesus who wants so much to please God. The wisdom and goodness that we have in ourselves comes from Christ. The weakness and blindness comes from Adam. In this process, Jesus takes onto himself all the blame for our sins. God no longer blames us for anything.

When Christ set off to do God's will, he fell way down into a woman's womb. The white smock the servant-Christ wore was his flesh, and shows that there is nothing that stands between God and humanity. The stains on the smock, the dirt and the raggedness of it, stand for Adam's hard work and struggle.

Then I saw the Son standing before God and saying, "See, God? I stand here before you in Adam's smock. I am ready to run to do whatever you want. I want to be on the earth to serve you, whenever you want to send me."

So the Son falls down into the woman's womb and the pain he suffered was that of taking on the body of a human being. He willingly endured all kinds of pain and misery during his time

on earth. By the servant's groaning and struggling in the ditch, I understood the beating, the shame, the pain of being murdered on the cross. When Christ, the servant, gave up his life on the cross, he put his soul and all humanity into God's hands.

Now God sits on a wondrous, noble throne in heaven, and the Son no longer stands there half-naked in his sweat-stained smock. The Son sits at God's right hand in endless peace.

Now let's be clear about this. I don't mean that the Son literally sits at God's right hand, as a man may sit at his wife's side. There's no such thing as sitting or standing in the Holy Trinity. Those are human words, but they are meant to show you the relationship between God and the Son.

And so the Son sits – fully God and fully human – in our soul, the city of rest and peace and endless joy.

❧ CHAPTER 51

G od is delighted to be our Father,
and God is delighted to be our Mother,
and God is delighted to be our true spouse
and our soul's beloved wife.
And Christ is delighted
to be our brother,
and Jesus is delighted to be our Savior.

These five wondrous joys are given to us, for our delight.

Our life is a marvelous mixture of sadness and delight. We have within ourselves the risen Christ, but also the pain of Adam's fall. In our dying, we are constantly protected by Christ. Touched by his grace, we are raised to salvation.

Because we are human – children of Adam – our emotions are conflicted with pain and darkness, so that it is hard to believe there can be such a thing as comfort. But there is another part of us that trusts God's mercy and grace, and our eyes are opened to that divine love. We live in this mixed-up state all our lives, but God wants us to trust the promise. God will be with us, in three ways.

Christ is with us in heaven,
the true human, who calls us upward.
Jesus is with us on earth,
leading us through life.
God is with us, in our soul,
living within us,
guiding and guarding.

So the story of the Lord and Servant showed us the pain, the blindness of our human state, symbolized by the fall of Adam. The

Lord in the story showed compassion and love for Adam – in other words, compassion for us. The Lord also showed us the power of Christ's death on the cross.

So it seems strange but true that God rejoices in the death of Christ, because without that, we would never know the fullness of the joy that we are given.

If, because of our blindness and stupidity, we mess up our lives, then let us stand up and change our lives, knowing that this sweet grace is within us. We can go on our way with God in love.

God wants us to be aware of our sin – to know that we have fallen and that many kinds of pain and suffering can come from this. On our own, we can't overcome our own weakness. And it doesn't matter. God wants us simply to be aware of the love, of the mercy that is there for us.

Pain and agony
are part of our being.
Endless love and forgiveness are part of our being.
Nothing separates them.
All are part of one love.

❦ CHAPTER 52

God takes our falling no harder than the fall of Adam, the first human. We know that Adam was loved and protected forever. God is good, gentle, kind, and can never assign complete failure to anyone.

When I learned this, I was partly satisfied that I had found an answer to my question. I learned that in every human soul there is an essential goodness that never desires anything evil, and wants to do nothing but good.

I realized that God never began to love humankind. There was no beginning.

> Before we were made,
> God loved us.
> When we were created,
> we loved God.
> And so our souls are made by God,
> and at the same moment, knit to God.

God created the human body out of the earth. In other words, our bodies were created out of something else. But God created the human soul out of nothing at all. From the very first, there was nothing that separated us from God. And so in that mysterious way, we are united with God.

We are held and protected in this endless love of God from the very beginning. And we shall continue to be joined with God in this knot of love for all eternity.

❧ CHAPTER 53

Because of the endless love that God has for all humanity, there is no difference between the soul of Christ and the soul of the lowest person on the social ladder.

So we should be happy that God lives in our soul, and even happier that our soul lives in God. Our soul was created to be God's home.

I saw no difference between our essential nature, and the nature of God. We are part of God and God is part of us.

The great universal truth of the Trinity is our Father,
who made us and who keeps us.
The deep wisdom of the Trinity is our Mother,
in whom we are all enclosed.
And the high goodness of the Trinity is our Lord,
in whom we are enclosed and who is enclosed in us.
We are enclosed in the Father,
and we are enclosed in the Son,
and we are enclosed in the Holy Spirit.
And the Father is enclosed in us,
and the Son is enclosed in us,
and the Holy Spirit is enclosed in us.
All Power!
All Wisdom!
All Goodness!
One God!
One Lord!

Through this power, working in us, we can be God's children, living Christian lives.

🎕 CHAPTER 54

God wants us to know – to understand – that we really are more at home in heaven than we are on earth. When our soul is breathed into our body, a body which is very human and sensual – at that moment, grace and love begin working in us. We are protected and cared for, as the Holy Spirit works in us all our lives. The Spirit grows in us, until we are returned again into the power of Christ, increased and fulfilled.

Our body, our sensuality, is our human nature. God is part of this body – this sensuousness. At the moment that God becomes part of this sensuality, our body becomes the city of God. God lives in this city and will never leave it.

And so God, through Christ,
becomes part of us.
Our soul and our body grow together,
body with soul
and soul with body,
each helping the other
until we have reached the fullness
of our human growth.
And then,
through God's creative nature,
we become all we are called to be,
the Holy Spirit again breathes grace into us,
and gives us the gift
that leads to eternal life.

Our human body, and the spirit of God within us, are really just one soul. The godly spirit was always there, and always at peace with God. Our human body, our sensuality, was there for us in the body of Christ, who suffered through that body for all of us.

That is what I saw in my vision – that soul and that body rejoicing together in the heart of God.

❧ CHAPTER 55

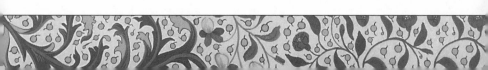

A nd so I saw very clearly that it is faster and easier to know God than it is to know our own soul. That is because our soul is grounded so deeply in God, and is so treasured by God, that we can never really know our own soul until we know God.

Even so, we have a natural and a deep need to know ourselves – our own souls. So we learn to look for our soul where it really is. In God! God is nearer to us than our own soul because God is the foundation on which our soul stands.

> Our soul rests in God,
> Our soul grows in God,
> Our soul is rooted in God's endless love.

In other words, if we want to know our own soul – our own selves – better, we must look for it in God, in whom it is embraced.

The fine city in which our Lord Jesus sits is our body, in which he is embraced. We may well yearn and feel ourselves unworthy until we are led so deeply into God that we find ourselves there.

❧ CHAPTER 56

Now about our essential nature.

God made us so noble and endowed us so richly, that we naturally, without holding back, strain to do what is pleasing to God. In our essential human nature, we *want* to live in God's way.

But in our bodily nature, we don't measure up as well. We seem unable to live the way God intended. Even so, by love and by grace, God makes up the difference for us.

This essential human nature was part of God's very being at the moment of creation. Our lower bodily nature became part of God in the incarnation of Christ. In other words, our two natures become one in Christ Jesus.

All of this was an act of divine love. When God was knitted into our bodily nature in Mary's womb, God took on a body like ours. Mary became, in a sense, our mother, in whom we were all enclosed when Christ was born out of her.

Jesus is then also our true mother in whose love we are carried, now and always.

❦ CHAPTER 57

G od, the blessed Trinity,
      is everlasting.
        Endless.
    Without beginning.

It was God's eternal purpose to create us. Our human nature was first created for Jesus, the second person of the Trinity.

God almighty is our natural father.
God all-wisdom is our natural mother.
Those two, along with the Holy Spirit,
        are all one God.

I saw, in the work of the Trinity, three characteristics or realities: fatherliness, motherliness, lordliness. All in one God!
    We experience our lives in three ways.

First we have our sense of being.
Then we have a sense of growing.
Third, we have a sense of fulfillment.
        The first is nature,
        the second is mercy,
        and the third is grace.
    The great strength of the Trinity
            is our father,
    the deep wisdom of the Trinity
            is our mother,
    and the great love of the Trinity
            is Christ.

We have all these in ourselves, naturally, through our essential nature. And so it is that in our father, God almighty, we have our being. In our tender mother, we are remade and restored. Our torn-apart lives are brought together into perfect humanity. Then, by giving ourselves into the care of the Holy Spirit, we are made whole.

> Our essence is our father, God almighty.
> Our essence is our mother, God all-wise.
> Our essence is the Holy Spirit, God all-goodness.

CHAPTER 58

The mercy and grace, which we experience in God, we would never have known unless it had been opposed. God allowed wickedness to rise in opposition to the goodness. God's goodness, mercy, and grace opposed that wickedness, and turned everything to goodness and honor for all of us.

The part of God that opposes evil is known to us through Christ. Like a mother, Christ protects us with love.

As surely as God is our father, so surely God is our mother. That is why God tells us,

"It is I.
It is I, the power and goodness of fatherhood.
It is I, the wisdom and love of motherhood.
It is I, the light and the grace that is love.
I am the Trinity.
I am the Unity.
I am the one who teaches you to love.
I am the one who makes you yearn for me.
I am the one who responds
to all your genuine desires."

God loved us and knew us before time began. Out of this love, God wanted the second person of the Trinity to be our mother, our brother, and our Savior. And so as truly as God is our father, so truly God is our mother.

Our father wills,
Our mother acts,
and the Holy Spirit confirms.

There are three ways to understand the motherhood of God. The first is the way in which our human nature was created through love. The second is the way in which God took our human nature and showed us this mothering love in Christ. And the third is seeing motherhood at work.

Everything in nature is suffused with that grace. And it is all one love.

CHAPTER 59

Now I need to say a little more about how God's mothering love brought us back to our essential human nature.

God, who is the mother of humanity, began the holy work of creating us in the womb of Mary. In this humble place, God put on human flesh, in order to become the mother of everything.

A mother's work is there with us, ready and dependable. No one could ever be such a mother except God.

We know that our mothers birthed us into pain and death. But our true mother Jesus, who is all love, gives us birth into joy and endless life. Jesus carried us in his womb of love, and when he had finished his work and carried us to full term, he brought us into life through the birth pangs of the crucifixion.

But after having done all this, Jesus still yearned to love us. He couldn't die on the cross again, but he would not stop working. He continues to nourish us with his love.

A mother will hold her child to her breast and feed the child with her milk. But our wonderful mother Jesus feeds us with himself, by giving us the food of life through the sacrament of communion.

The word "mother" is such a tender and gentle word that we can't really use it to describe anyone except God, who is the mother of all life and all creation.

A kind and loving mother knows what her child needs. She protects and helps the child, because that is the nature of being a mother. When her child gets older, she changes the way she does her mothering, but she never changes her love. She even allows the child to be hurt sometimes, because that is the way children grow.

The debt we owe to God for this gracious love we repay by loving God as both mother and father.

❧ CHAPTER 60

As we are being spiritually born in this way, Christ protects us tenderly – more tenderly than we can imagine, because we are so precious.

Christ kindles our understanding,
guides us on our journey,
eases our conscience,
comforts our soul,
and lightens our heart.

And yet, Christ allows some of us to fall and hurt ourselves more than we ever did before. We begin to think that our faith in Christ is for nothing.

That's not the way it is. We need to fall. We need to know we have fallen, because if we didn't fall we'd develop an inflated sense of who we really are, and how little we know or understand. If we didn't fall, we might never know the wonderful love of our creator.

A mother sometimes allows her child to fall, or make mistakes, or do things that are not wise or useful. But she'll never allow any permanent injury to happen. A mother sometimes watches her own child die, but our mother Jesus will never allow a child to die except in the sense of an earthly death.

Sometimes when we mess up, we work ourselves into such a state that we are afraid and ashamed and we don't know what to do with ourselves. When a small child feels this way, it runs to mother and says, "Oh mom! I've made myself filthy again. I can't clean myself up except with your help."

If we run to Christ in this way, even though we haven't got ourselves back together again, it is because Christ is behaving like a wise mother. Sometimes it is good for us to live with our mess-ups for a while, until we are genuinely ready to change things in our life.

Christ will never abandon us.

The flood of Christ's mercy, symbolized by the flow of blood and water when he was dying on the cross, is enough to make us clean and whole again. The tender hands of Christ, our mother, are always there for us, like a kind nurse whose whole duty it is to take care of us.

> It is Christ's work to save us.
> It is Christ's honor to help us.
> It is Christ's will that we know this.

CHAPTER 61

God has revealed to us our frailty, our failings, our betrayals, denials, hatred – in other words, the load of sin we carry around with us. But at the same time, I was shown God's power, wisdom, and love. God keeps us when we face these difficult times, just as God keeps us in those times when we are at peace with ourselves and with others.

God is the very essence of nature. In fact, the goodness which is nature, is God, the ground, the essence of nature. God is the same thing as nature. God is the true father and mother of all of nature.

We don't need to search high and low for those vital powers that come to us from God. We look to the church. And we look into our own soul. In those two places we will find all that we need.

❧ CHAPTER 62

It is human nature to hate sin.

Human nature is good and worthy, and God's grace was sent to protect human nature and to destroy sin.

When, through God's grace, we grow into harmony with both our human nature and grace, we find out that sin is more awful and far more painful than hell. Sin is not only impure, it is *unnatural*. It is a frightful thing to see – when a soul is given over to sin – a soul that should be shining and beautiful in the sight of God. Sin is the opposite of human nature.

Still, we can go to the mother we love so much and our souls will be made pliant and gentle. Our mother will restore us to health. God will never stop working until all human children are born through Christ's crucifixion, because, in taking on our human nature, God restored life to us and birthed us into endless life.

Then we will understand what God means with these words: "All shall be well. And you will see for yourself, that all manner of thing shall be well."

❦ CHAPTER 63

Many times I had a deep longing to die – to have done with this world. There is so much suffering and pain, compared to the joy of heaven. So often, I felt miserable, depressed, and weak. I didn't want to live and suffer that way.

And then God answered me.

"Suddenly,
you will be taken away from your pain,
from all your sickness,
from all your depression,
from all of your fear.
And you will come up to me,
and our reunion will be your reward.
You will be filled with love and happiness.
There will be no more pain,
no more unhappiness, no more depression.
You will have joy and happiness without end."

Then I saw in my vision a body lying on the ground. It was bloated and horrible and stinking. Out of that body came a beautiful child, lively and smiling, and I saw it glide smoothly up to heaven.

I understood that the stinking, swollen body represented our life with all its struggle and pain and evil. And the child represented our souls, clean and pure and beautiful.

It is much better that we be taken away from our pain, rather than to have our pain taken from us. And then I again heard God's words.

"You shall come to me,
and you will no longer be in pain.
I will answer all your needs,
and you will be filled with joy and happiness."

We must accept God's will and consolation as fully as we possibly can, and take our sufferings and our pain as lightly as we can. If we can take our pain lightly, then those pains won't seem as important or as destructive to us. And God will bless us in this struggle.

CHAPTER 64

I realized that if we choose to live in the love of God, we can be sure that we are always loved and that grace will work within us.

God wants me to feel that everything done through Christ was done for *me* particularly! And so you should feel that everything God has done, was done for just *you*! Personally! God brings us into such a sense of unity with everyone we can never stand apart and disconnected from the rest of humanity.

And so it happens that even though we may be in such pain and distress that we can't think of anything else, we can quickly get to the other side of that agony, realizing that it really wasn't as bad as we thought.

Why?
God wants us to know
how much we are loved,
and in that knowledge
we will find
peace and rest.

That's why God gave me these words: "Why should you be upset that you have struggles to endure. You need that experience in order to grow spiritually."

❦ CHAPTER 65

Before I go on, I need to confess to you my own weakness and my own blindness. I began to feel that I wouldn't die, that I would live, and after a while my sickness came back. I felt it first in my head where I seemed to have a dreadful clatter – a noise. Then my whole body was sick, the way it had been before.

I felt barren and dry as if I'd never had any of those wonderful visions. I moaned and cried because I hurt so much and there seemed to be no spiritual or physical help for me.

Then a priest came to me and asked me how I was feeling. I told him I had been raving. He laughed out loud.

Then I said to him, "The crucifix that I was looking at – I thought it was bleeding."

When I said this, the priest's face became very sober and I felt really ashamed of the way I had been talking. I realized this man was taking what I said very seriously, so I didn't say anything more. I was terribly upset. I wanted to say my confession, but I thought, "Why would a priest believe me? Even I didn't believe what I was shown by God."

I had believed what God showed me, and I thought I would believe it forever, but then, like a fool, I forgot all about it. Just because I felt a bit of pain, I had lost all the comfort and reassurance that God had showed me. You see what kind of person I am?

But even then, my gentle God didn't leave me. So I lay quietly on my bed, trusting in God's mercy. Then I fell asleep.

In my sleep, the Devil came and took me by the throat, pushing himself right in my face. He was like a very thin, ugly young man. His hair was rusty red and he grinned at me, showing me his white teeth. It was horrible. He didn't have a real body or hands, but he put his paws on my throat and tried to strangle me, but he couldn't.

But in all this, I was able to trust and be saved by God's love. Then I woke up and my mother, who was with me, wet my temples and I began to feel better.

Then I fell asleep again and dreamed that smoke was coming through the door, and with it came heat and a foul stench. I woke up and shouted, "Blessed be God! Is everything on fire here?" The people who were with me said, "No, there's no fire here."

So again I said, "Blessed be God!" I knew that the Devil was trying to tempt me.

I kept myself focused on all the things God had showed me that day, and on the faith I had been taught in my church, because to me they were the same thing. I kept my thoughts on that, and soon all the smoke and the stink was gone, and I felt rested and comfortable. My sickness and my fear were gone.

❧ CHAPTER 66

Then God opened my inner eye and showed me my own soul, which was in my heart. My soul, it seemed, was as big as the world – a peaceable kingdom. In the center of that glorious city sat our Lord Jesus, who was strong and honorable and majestic.

The place that Jesus takes for his dwelling is our soul. He will live there forever.

God knew from the beginning what would please our Lord Jesus, that nothing would be fit to be his dwelling place except the human soul, and that is why we were created. God made us for Christ's dwelling place – made us better, more noble, more beautiful than any other creature.

God wants us to rejoice in that reality and lift our hearts above the pains and struggles we experience.

❧ CHAPTER 67

This was a delightful sight and a restful vision. God is very pleased if we realize this, because the soul that sees Christ in this way becomes one with Christ.

Then Christ spoke to me, even though I heard no voice.

> "Be reassured.
> You were not raving.
> Take the gift
> and believe it.
> Hold on to it firmly.
> Be comforted by it.
> Trust it
> and you will not be overcome!"

These words were not spoken just for *me*. They were spoken for *all* of us, so that we might have strength to deal with the pain and sorrow that we will encounter in this life.

God didn't say,

> "You won't be tempted.
> You won't suffer pain.
> You will not be depressed."
> God did say,
> "You shall not be overcome."

God wants us to hear those words, to believe them, and to find our strength in them.

God loves us.
God delights in us.
We are made
to love and delight in God –
to trust in God,
and then indeed,
all shall be well.

❧ CHAPTER 68

That night the Devil came again with his heat and his stink. That got me fearfully upset, because the stink was so vile and painful. Then I heard a chattering sound – something like two people having a heated conversation, though I couldn't understand what they said. It seemed to me they were ridiculing the way some people say their prayers, mechanically, without thought or devotion.

I felt a sense of despair, but I kept my eyes focused on the cross. I spoke words about Christ's crucifixion, and words I had learned from my church, and I kept my heart fixed on God with all the trust and strength I could find.

That's the way the Devil kept me busy all night. But in the morning the evil was all gone, although I could still smell the stink he left behind. As Jesus said before, "That is the way the Devil is overcome."

❧ CHAPTER 69

The vision seemed to be fading and I had no signal – no token that might help me keep the vision. But God did give words to remember and hold in my heart.

> "Keep yourself in the faith.
> Find comfort in the faith.
> Trust yourself to the faith."

And so I am determined to keep my faith, even though I was stupid enough to let it slip away at that time. But God continues to be gracious and good, showing me the visions again in my soul. That showing was more beautiful, more profound than the first showing. Again I heard the words:

> "Know this well.
> You were not raving.
> Take this faith
> and keep yourself there.
> Believe it.
> Comfort yourself with it.
> You will not be overcome."

CHAPTER 70

F aith is a delightful, cheerful sweet thing.

God looks at us continually and wants to give us that sense of inward joy – that longing and that love which seeps into our souls.

In our time of pain and despair, God shows us the passion of Jesus on the cross, and so is able to keep us from all our enemies. God showed this to me so that we might move through our lives with a sense of joy and a holy presence.

❧ CHAPTER 71

Now I need to tell you how it is that we sometimes see deadly sin in those who live in the joy of God.

I saw two opposites. The highest joy and the deepest pain.

The highest joy because we have a clear knowledge of God. We feel the fullness of God's love. The deepest pain we can ever experience is the emptiness we feel when we become aware of our own sinfulness.

In our struggle with these two opposites, there are thoughts that make us laugh and those that make us cry. Joyful laughter because God, our Creator, is so near to us and in us that we can live happily in that sheer goodness. But we cry because we find ourselves too weighed down by our humanity, by our sin, that we may never see that sheer, holy goodness.

So we find ourselves continually weeping, not necessarily tears from our eyes, but the inward weeping, the yearning of our soul for that unity with God, until the natural desire of our soul is so great, so penetrating, that we see again the face of our Creator.

We might suffer all the pain and distress imaginable, but when we see God's face the pain and distress will no longer injure us.

So it is good to have three kinds of wisdom.

The first, that we know God.
The second, that we know ourselves
and the way in which God made us
and lives in us.
The third, we realize that our essential self,
our soul, doesn't want to sin.

It seems to me that all my visions came to teach me those three things.

❦ CHAPTER 72

God showed me two kinds of spiritual sickness from which we suffer.

The first one is impatience or laziness.
The other is despair or fear.

God showed me sin, in the general sense – all the things humans do to injure themselves and to hurt others. But I was shown these two sins, impatience and fear, particularly. Those of us who love God struggle the most against these two. They upset us most deeply. People who genuinely love God and want to live a wholesome, spiritual life are the ones who are most susceptible to these two sins.

God wants us to get to know these, so we can avoid them as we do the other sins.

Some of us believe
that God is all powerful and can do everything.
Some of us believe
that God is all-wisdom and can do everything.
But we stop there.
That God is all love and *wishes* to do everything –
that we refuse to believe.
It is this ignorance
that most hinders
those who love God.

Sometimes we mistake this fear for humility, but it is a blindness and a weakness. We can't avoid it the way we avoid other kinds of sin, because it is so subtle. Our generous God forgives our sins before we even think of them. But God also wants us to repent and change our ways.

And – this is important – God also wants us to forgive *ourselves* when we succumb to depression and fear.

❦ CHAPTER 73

We experience fear in four ways.

First, there's the fear of being attacked in some way, which we experience because we feel weak and frail. This is a good kind of fear, because it's a cleansing of the spirit, much as some of the sickness and pain we feel. This kind of fear, if we recognize and accept it, can be part of our spiritual growth.

The second fear is of pain, especially the fear of death, which can wake us up, if we are spiritually asleep. Those asleep in this way don't recognize the tender love of God, until they begin to feel the gentle mercy of God. This kind of fear can actually be of help to us.

The third fear is doubt. This fear can pull us down into despair. The bitterness of doubt can be changed into the sweetness of a natural and healthy trust in God.

The fourth is reverent fear – the only kind of fear which God wants us to experience. It is a soft fear. The more you experience this fear, the less painful it is because of the sweetness of God's love.

Love and fear are siblings. They are part of the way we were created and we will always have them with us.

At the center of our being, we all want to love God gently, humbly, and powerfully. When we fear God, in the kind and gentle way that we experience God, then our time of worship will be so much more vigorous. If we don't have a reverent fear of God and a genuine love of God, worship will be meaningless.

So let's express our fears to God and pray for that reverent fear and gentle love that is God's gift.

❦ CHAPTER 74

I saw in my vision that God can do all that is necessary for us. And there are three things that we need.

We need love;
we need a yearning for God;
and we need compassion.
Love and compassion protect us.
Our yearning draws us into heaven.
As we yearn for God,
so God yearns for us.
God thirsts for us.
God longs to have union with all humanity.
Until that is fully accomplished, God thirsts.
God thirsts for us
as we thirst for God.

There are so many great gifts God has yearned to give us from the beginning of time. We're simply not ready to receive all these gifts now. When we do receive them, heaven and earth will quake with the sheer wonder of it all.

Thinking about this makes us gentle and humble, and that is why God wants us to yearn for the gift. This reverent fear leads us in the right direction and unites us with God.

❧ CHAPTER 75

I hope you will understand that I don't say much about reverent fear because God didn't show me anyone who didn't already have this yearning.

If you genuinely accept the teaching of the Holy Spirit, you will be much more concerned about the misery and hopelessness that sin causes than you will be about any thoughts of hell. God wants us to earnestly seek to learn the ways of God so that we do not fall into sin.

Avoid getting yourself involved in other people's sinfulness, because that becomes a smoke screen that makes it harder to see yourself and your own journey of faith.

In this vision, I saw two opposites – deepest wisdom and the highest folly. In this wisdom we live out our lives in the counsel of our highest Friend, Jesus. We will always be held in his love and compassion, even when our lives become soiled with pain and distress. Then, because of our own stupidity, we see ourselves as wretched, blind, and unfaithful. We often promise to do better, but we keep falling into the same trap, over and over.

We become afraid of God. Our Enemy stimulates this kind of fear by threatening us with the anger of God. He wants us to feel so weighed down, so tired, that we are afraid to pray to our Everlasting Friend.

It is our Enemy who tries to hold us back in our journey of faith – who wants us to be filled with fear and so depressed that we never come into the gentle presence of our Friend Jesus.

֍ CHAPTER 76

Then, in my vision, God showed me the Devil. I learned that everything that is in opposition to love and peace comes from that fiend. If we flail around in our human weakness, then the Devil rejoices. If we rise above it, and give ourselves into the embracing love of God, the Devil burns with envy.

So this is the remedy. Know yourself and acknowledge your weakness. Then quickly put yourself into the care of Christ. Say to yourself,

> "God is almighty and may punish me harshly.
> God is all wisdom and will punish me wisely.
> God is all goodness and loves me tenderly."

I wasn't shown any particular punishment for specific sins. But I was shown that we need to bear the pains and distresses of our human life – to see them as God's way of helping us to grow. For God said,

> "Don't accuse yourself too much,
> thinking that your struggle and your pain
> is all your fault.
> It's not my will
> that you be depressed and guilt ridden.
> Because, whatever you do,
> you will encounter pain.
> I want you to know
> that through your faithful living
> you will grow in love."

This life sometimes feels like a prison. All our struggles and pain feel like God's punishment. But God wants us to know that we will find joy in our faithfulness. God will protect us and bring us joy in this life.

❦ CHAPTER 77

Our merciful God helps us to see our sin and our inadequacy by shining the light of divine mercy on us.

There are four things about our sin that God wants us to understand.

First, that God is our foundation, out of which we have our very life, our being.

Second, God protects us even when we are sinning, even when we are at our lowest and most miserable.

Third, that God is gentle with us, even though we go astray.

And fourth, that God stays with us and thinks no less of us. God wants us to come back – to be one with God, as God is one with us.

Because of this gentle way in which God shows us how we mess up our lives, we can see our own error without a sense of despair. We will see ourselves as we really are, which is necessary for our spiritual growth.

Sometimes we find it very hard to see ourselves that way, because we may find ourselves more sinful and more destructive than we had ever imagined. But God very carefully lets us see just as much as we can handle. In that way, we can break away from all that is destructive in our lives and discover that our Savior heals us and draws us back into God's loving arms.

This is knowledge we can never gain by trying to understand things ourselves. God is ready to help us grow and we will be grateful to God who, with mercy and grace, showed us ourselves.

❧ CHAPTER 78

When God showed me how I would sin, I thought it was only me that sinned. But God wants all humanity to understand this. God has enough love for every human being, even though we all sin.

In fact, I was shown that I should not worry about other people's sins unless there was some way that I could help them or comfort them.

In all this I learned that God's love is endless and unchanging and that we can never be separated from that love. Our gentle God touches us, stirs us, calls us, and wants us to see ourselves as we really are, so that we can be reunited to the one who heals us and gives us life.

❧ CHAPTER 79

We are able to endure this life because of three things.

The first is our natural reason.
The second is the church.
The third is the working of the Holy Spirit.
These three are really just one God.

God is the foundation of our reason. God comes to us through the teachings of the church. God is the Holy Spirit working in us. All three of these always work together in us.

Because of our faith, we know that God took our nature in Christ Jesus. He lives in us and guides us and brings us joy. Christ will keep on working as long as there is a single soul left on earth that has not been brought into unity with God.

I know that clergy sometimes talk to us about angels. I can't argue with that, but angels were not shown to me in my vision. It is Christ who does everything for us – everything we need for this life on earth and when we come to heaven.

Christ's love never allows him to be without pity. When we get our lives messed up and we feel unworthy, when we become tired or depressed, then Christ carries the whole burden for us.

Christ is here with us. Christ is here because of us and *only* because of us. And though we may feel very alone in our sinfulness, God never lets us be alone, because Christ forgives us and protects us from blame.

❦ CHAPTER 80

G od has chosen no other place to live except in our souls.

This dwelling that God has chosen in our souls is beautiful and stately. There, God touches us and rejoices in our love far more than sorrowing over our failings. God wants us to live gladly and cheerfully, even though this life sometimes feels like a punishment.

God wants us to look beyond the pain that we feel to the joy we can trust.

❦ CHAPTER 81

God helped me understand the pain and grief that is part of life.

> "I know that you live for my love,
> gladly and cheerfully enduring
> the struggles of life.
> Since you can't live without sin,
> you are ready to suffer for my love
> all the agony, confusion, and depression
> that may come to you.
> That's the reality of life.
> But try not to be depressed about sin
> that you can't avoid."

Then I remembered the parable of the Lord and the Servant. The Lord looked on the servant with pity, not with blame. God loves us always, yet we sin continually. But if we hold on tight to the love of God, which we have experienced, we will realize that this love is the remedy for all our troubles.

> "I love you
> and you love me
> and our love will never be separated.
> It is for your sake
> that I suffer."

If there is a person in this world who has never made a mistake, such a person was not shown to me. But whether we are falling or standing up (and all of us do both), we are always held in God's love.

It is important that we see both these things at once. God wants us to keep thinking of the higher love – of the way we are when we are deeply aware of God's love. But we are not to forget that we also

fall and hurt ourselves and others badly. This will continually happen to us, until we are fully aware that we have Jesus as our reward and we are filled with joy.

CHAPTER 82

There are three ways we can describe God.

God is life.

God is love.

God is light.

In life, is a wonderful sense of belonging.

In love, is a gentle kindness.

In light, is our endless human nature.

Our faith comes to us in our human nature as light – an endless day through God our father. In that light, our mother Christ and the Holy Spirit lead us through life.

This light gives us life, but it is the night that causes our pain and our depression. By God's mercy and grace we can walk confidently in that light.

In other words, our faith is our light in the darkness – a light that is God.

❧ CHAPTER 83

That light is love.

This love isn't bright enough to see what God has promised us in the next life. It is enough light that we can live faithfully and do the work that brings honor to God.

I had three ways of understanding this love.

Uncreated love is God.
Created love is our soul in God.
Love given is a virtue.

Love given is a gift of God's grace and is expressed by the way we live our lives. Through that, we find ourselves simply in love with God. We find ourselves in God and in everything that loves God.

All of this we do for God's sake.

❦ CHAPTER 84

I shook my head in wonder when I had that vision.

Because even with all our stupidity and blindness, God looks at us and rejoices. God is pleased with us. God is most pleased with us when we believe and enjoy this great divine love – when we find joy being with God and living in God.

We will find joy forever in the love of God and we will know that we have existed in the heart of God since before the beginning of time.

> In this love, God made us.
> In this love, God keeps us.
> God will never allow us to be hurt
> in a way that would destroy this joy.

When the end of time comes and we all live in the company of God, we will see clearly and understand fully the mysteries that now perplex us. None of us will need to say, "Lord, if it had been this way or that, then everything would have been just fine."

Instead, we will all say together with one voice,

> "This is the way it is,
> and that is the way it should be,
> and it is well."

Then we will see that everything that has happened was planned by God from the beginning of time.

❧ CHAPTER 85

For the sake of love, let us all thank, trust, and enjoy God. Because God said to me, "I am at the root of your yearning."

I saw and understood this meaning – that we will be given grace to love and to cling to God. We are God's holy treasure, seen with such a holy love. God wants to do nothing more than to give us more light, more spiritual joy, more comfort.

Over the course of 15 years, I often wanted to know God's meaning. What does God want us to do with our lives? Then I received this answer:

"Would you know our Lord's meaning in all this?
Learn it well.
Love was the meaning.
Who showed it to you?
Love.
What did God show you?
Love.
Why did God show it to you?
For love.
Hold fast to this and you shall learn
and know more about love.
But you shall never learn anything
except love from God."

So I was taught that love was our Lord's meaning. And I saw full surely that before ever God made us, God loved us. This love was never quenched, nor ever shall be.

And in this love
God has created everything that is.
And in this love
God has made all things for our benefit.
In this love is our life everlasting.
All this shall we see in God without end –
which Jesus grant us.
Amen.

CHAPTER 86

Some resources to enrich your appreciation of Julian of Norwich

There's more material about Julian of Norwich than any one person can read, much less digest. If you go to the website www.joinhands.com, you will find a number of resources to aid your study of Julian.

If you are fortunate enough to live near Norwich, England, or can travel there, the Friends of Julian operate a fine Resource Centre right next to St. Julian's Church. You can become a "Friend of Julian" or reach the Resource Centre at Rouen Road, Norwich, NR1 1QT, England. The e-mail address is friendsofjulian@ukgateway.net.

In the USA, the Order of Julian of Norwich (Anglican) stocks books and other resources related to Julian. They can be reached at 2812 Summit Ave., Waukesha, WI, 53188. The e-mail address is ordjulian@aol.com.

Old hands and "new hands" who have just discovered Julian can join Ralph Milton at an online chat group that has the same name as his novel. It is called *Julian's Cell*. To become part of this discussion, go to www.joinhands.com, click on *Ralph's Resource Barrel*, and just follow the prompts.

If you are new to the subject of Julian of Norwich, Ralph Milton's historical novel, *Julian's Cell: an earthy story of Julian of Norwich* is the

best place to begin. Following that, this book, *The Essence of Julian* would be appropriate.

That could be followed by one or both of these excellent books by Sheila Upjohn.

- *In Search of Julian of Norwich*, by Sheila Upjohn. London: Darton, Longman & Todd, Ltd., 1995.
- *Why Julian Now? A Voyage of Discovery*, by Sheila Upjohn. London: Darton, Longman & Todd, Ltd., London, 1997.

There are a number of translations of Julian's work which you might wish to pursue when you've read this one.

Here are some of the better translations.

- *All Shall Be Well*, a translation by Sheila Upjohn. Harrisburg, PA: Morehouse Publishing, 1992. Of the various translations of Julian's *Showings*, this is easily the most readable.
- *Julian of Norwich Showings*, by Edmund Colledge and James Walsh. Mahwah, NJ: Paulist Press, 1978. Regarded by some as the most scholarly translation, this book contains a good commentary on Julian, both her Short and Long texts, and a helpful concordance.
- *Revelation of Love*, by John Skinner. New York: An Image Book, 1997. Also quite readable.
- *Lesson of Love*, by Fr. John-Julian is a readable and scholarly translation. It is available through the Order of Julian of Norwich (address above).
- *Julian of Norwich: Revelations of Divine Love*, by Clifton Wolters. New York: Penguin Books, 1966.
- *Julian of Norwich: Revelations & Motherhood of God* by Frances Beer. Cambridge: D. S. Brewer, 1998. This book contains a translation of the *Short Text*, and the "mothering God" chapters from the *Long Text*.

Various commentators have published books of theological commentary on Julian's writings. Two of the most useful are

- *Julian of Norwich* by Grace Jantzen. London: SPCK, 2000.
- *Julian of Norwich's Showings* by Denise Nowakowski Baker. Princeton: Princeton University Press, 1994.

Below are some useful resources that will give you a fuller understanding of the times in which Julian lived.

- *The Book of Margery Kempe*, trans. by B. A. Windeatt. New York: Penguin Books, 1985.
- *Memoirs of a Medieval Woman*: *The Life and Times of Margery Kempe*, Louise Collis. New York: Harper & Row, 1983.
- *Margery Kempe of Lynn and Medieval England*, by Margaret Gallyon. Norwich: The Canterbury Press, 1995.
- *Women in Medieval Society*, by Mavis E. Mate. Cambridge: Cambridge University Press, 1999.
- *Medieval Women* by Eileen Power. Cambridge: Cambridge University Press, 1975.
- *Women and Mystical Experiences in the Middle Ages*, by Frances Beer. Suffolk, England: The Boydell Press, 1992.
- *Visions and Longings: Medieval Women Mystics* by Monica Furlong. London: Shambhala Publications, 1996.
- *Brides in the Desert; the Spirituality of the Beguines* by Saskia Murk-Jansen. Maryknoll, NY: Orbis Books, 1998. Note: some scholars claim that Julian was a Beguine before she became an anchorite.
- *Ancrene Wisse: Guide for Anchoresses*, trans. by Hugh White. New York: Penguin Books, 1993.
- *Piers Plowman*, an alliterative verse translation, by E. Talbot Donaldson. New York: W. W. Norton & Company, 1990.

- *The Cloud of Unknowing*, ed. by Halcyon Backhouse. London: Hodder and Stoughton, 1985.
- *The Practice of the Presence of God* by Brother Lawrence of the Resurrection, trans. by John J. Delaney. New York: An Image Book, 1977.
- *Richard Rolle: the English Writings*, trans. by Rosamund S. Allen. Mahwah, NJ: Paulist Press, 1988.
- *The Canterbury Tales,* by Geoffrey Chaucer, a verse translation by David Wright. Oxford: Oxford University Press, 1985.
- *Meditations with Julian of Norwich*, by Brenden Doyle. Santa Fe, NM: Bear and Co., 1983.